# THE STORY OF BENJAMIN FRANKLIN

## A Biography Book for New Readers

Written by
**Shannon Anderson**

Illustrated by
**Steffi Walthall**

ROCKRIDGE PRESS

**Dedicated to all of my professors and former classmates from Franklin College**



For general information on our other products and services or to obtain technical support, please contact our Customer Care Department within the United States at (866) 744-2665, or outside the United States at (510) 253-0500.

Rockridge Press publishes its books in a variety of electronic and print formats. Some content that appears in print may not be available in electronic books, and vice versa.



Series Designer: Angela Navarra
Interior and Cover Designer: Lisa Schreiber
Art Producer: Hannah Dickerson
Editor: Orli Zuravicky
Production Editor: Mia Moran
Illustrations © 2020 Steffi Walthall. Photography © GeorgiosArt/iStock.com, p. 50; duncan1890/iStock.com, p. 52; Asar Studios/Alamy Stock Photo, p. 53. All maps used under license from Creative Market. Illustrator photo courtesy of Clarence Goss.

ISBN: Print 978-1-64739-821-7 | eBook 978-1-64739-495-0

R0

Printed in China

# CONTENTS

# CHAPTER 1

# AN AMERICAN LEGEND IS BORN

## Meet Benjamin Franklin

More than 300 years ago, Benjamin Franklin was born in a house on Milk Street in Boston, Massachusetts. From an early age, he loved learning, helping others, and problem-solving. He had a lot of big ideas. Those ideas led to many **inventions** that completely changed our world. We have Benjamin Franklin to thank for the **lightning rod**, bifocal glasses, and the Franklin stove. He even helped open the first post office, hospital, fire station, and library in America!

**JUMP IN THE THINK TANK**

How do you think people fought fires before there were fire stations?

Ben was always coming up with clever ways to make things better. As a young boy, Ben loved to swim. So he made wooden paddles to help him swim faster. Once he even used a kite to pull himself quickly through the water. Another

time, Ben and his friends were getting muddy while fishing. He built a wharf out of rocks for them to stand on. Ben's adventures throughout life taught him many lessons. He learned how to be careful with money, to never give up, and to find ways to improve how things worked. He did all of this with a good sense of humor. Ben loved making people laugh.

One of Ben Franklin's biggest accomplishments was helping create the United States of America. He was a **Founding Father** and helped form the **government** we have today. Ben also helped write the **Declaration of Independence** and the **Constitution of the United States**. These are both very important documents that helped America become a free and successful nation.

His hard work and big thinking made him a **legend** in his time. It is no wonder his face is on America's one-hundred-dollar bill!

## Benjamin's America

When Benjamin was born on January 17, 1706, America was not a country. It was made up of just 13 **colonies**. A colony is land that is controlled by another country. England controlled the 13 colonies. People came over from England and other places looking for a new life where they could make their own choices and belong to different religions.

Ben lived in Boston, Massachusetts—one of the biggest cities in the British colonies. It was a

popular place because it was a **port** city. People could sail there to trade goods or to find a place to live.

> "Early to bed, early to rise, makes a man healthy, wealthy, and wise."

Life in the colonies was hard. Families were large, and most homes only had one or two rooms. At this time in history, men and women had specific jobs to do. Most men worked on farms, or were skilled in a trade like metalworking, or making goods like barrels or shoes. Men worked all day and into the night. Women raised the kids, prepared meals, worked in the garden, and sewed clothes. Many children who attended school only went for a few years because they were expected to help on the farm or in the home.

Ben kept busy helping his family, learning about different kinds of jobs, and exploring with his friends. His father, Josiah, wanted

Ben to grow up to be a preacher in a church, but Ben had other ideas. Let's find out how his childhood helped shape Benjamin Franklin's amazing life as an inventor, scientist, writer, and Founding Father!

**WHEN?**

**1684** — Josiah Franklin arrives in Boston from England.

**1706** — Benjamin Franklin is born on January 17.

# CHAPTER 2

# THE EARLY YEARS

## Growing Up in the Colonies

Most families at the time were large, but Ben's was extra-large! He had nine brothers and seven sisters. Before long, the Franklin family grew too big for their house on Milk Street and had to move. Josiah made soap and candles, so part of the new house became Josiah's soap and candle shop.

When Ben was eight years old, he started school. Benjamin was great at writing but did not do well in arithmetic.

**MYTH & FACT**

**MYTH:** Ben was a vegetarian for his entire life.

**FACT:** Ben stopped eating meat at age 16 and was a vegetarian on and off during his life.

Two years later, he stopped going to school because his family couldn't afford it. Ben didn't stop learning, though. He took every chance he could to read books and saved money to buy them! He loved reading poetry, funny stories, and books about science.

In the 1700s, boys usually worked as **apprentices** to learn a trade, or skill. Apprentices weren't paid—instead, they were given food and a place to live. Apprentices usually worked for their employers until they were 21 years old. When Ben was 10 years old, he began to work in his father's candle shop.

Ben didn't like working in the candle shop. It was hot, and the animal fat used to make the candles stank. Ben was bored. He wanted a job that let him use his mind. His dream at the time was to become a sailor. Unfortunately, one of Ben's older brothers had been lost at sea, so his father didn't approve of sailing as a trade for Ben. After two years in the shop, Ben's father finally decided to let Ben try a different trade.

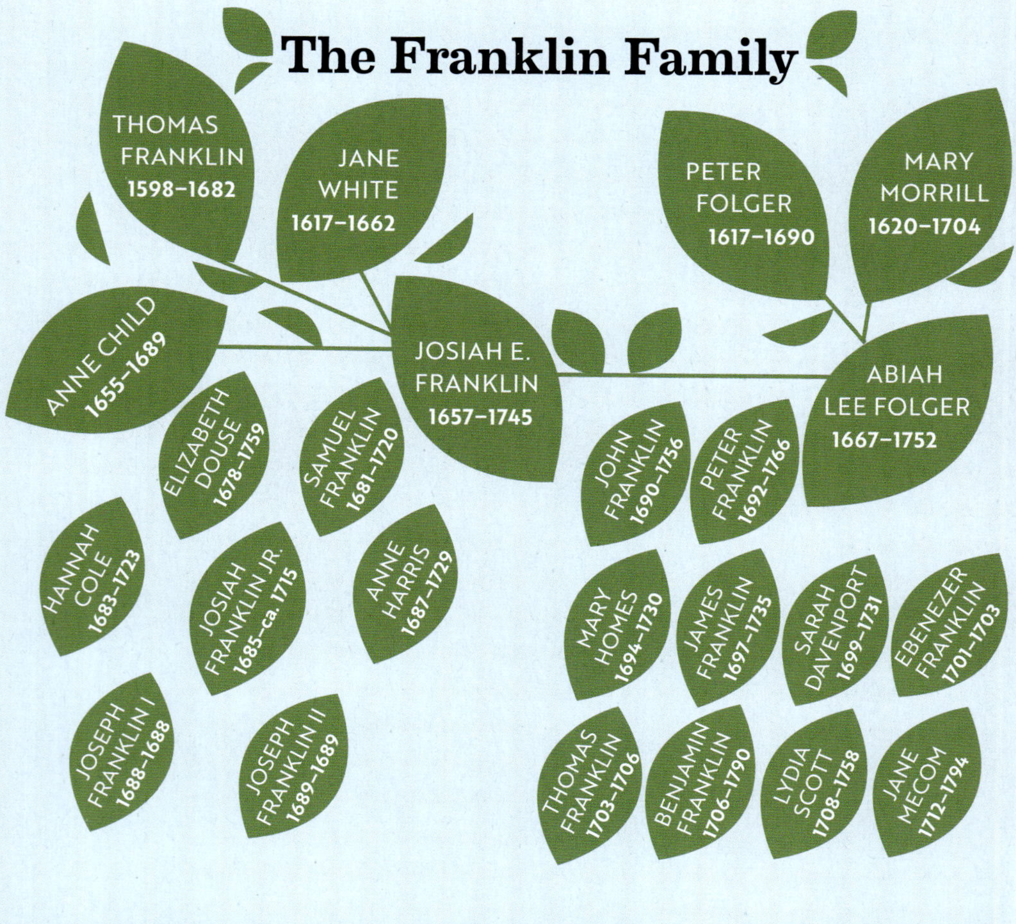

**JUMP —IN THE— THINK TANK**

Do you think it was fair that apprentices had to work for no pay?

Ben's father took him on walks through the city. Ben watched people build with bricks, make furniture, create pottery, and craft silverware. He loved watching them work, but he didn't find anything he wanted to do as his future job.

Josiah knew Ben loved books and words, so he let him work for James, Ben's older brother. James was a printer, and he owned a printing press. A printing press is a machine that is used to print pictures or words onto paper. At 12 years old, Ben was hopeful this would be a job he would enjoy, so off he went!

## Printer's Apprentice

Ben learned his job at the printing press quickly. He enjoyed setting up the print blocks to put inked letters on paper, but what he really wanted to do was write. Ben sometimes wrote poetry and stories in his free time, but he knew his brother would not print them. James mostly printed newspapers, essays, and posters. James also thought Ben was too young to have his work printed. James was often strict with Ben so the other workers wouldn't think he was making things easy for his brother.

Still, Ben wasn't ready to give up. He came up with a clever idea to get his work **published**.

He wrote funny stories about life in Boston and then slid them under the door of the print shop before it opened. Ben didn't sign his own name. He tricked his brother by making up a fake

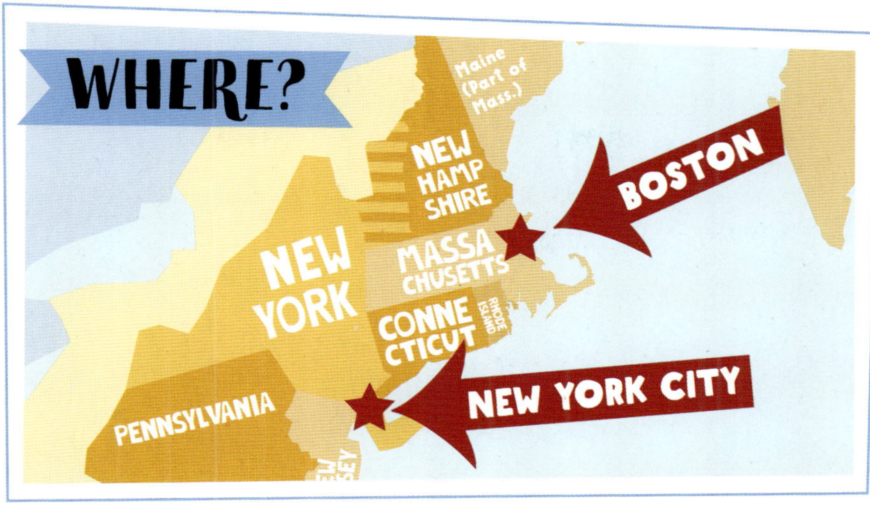


name that belonged to a fake woman—Silence Dogood. James found the stories and liked them. He decided to publish them! Ben's trick worked. People bought the papers and loved the stories, so Ben kept writing them. Months later, when Ben finally told his brother that *he* was Silence Dogood, James was very angry about being tricked.

James hadn't been a kind boss to his little brother. After finding out Ben was Silence Dogood, James was even worse. James was so mean that Ben didn't want to finish the apprenticeship. He was supposed to work for James for another four years, but when he was 17, Ben ran away. He boarded a ship for New York City and didn't look back.

## WHEN?

**1714** — Ben starts school at age eight.

**1716** — Ben begins work in his father's soap and candle shop.

**1718** — Ben begins working for his brother James at the print shop.

**1722** — Ben begins writing as Silence Dogood.

**1723** — Ben boards a boat to New York City.

# CHAPTER 3

# NEW BEGINNINGS

## City of Brotherly Love

In 1723, it took three days to sail from Boston to New York City on a ship. After his journey, Ben could not find a job in New York City. Once again, he set off—this time to Philadelphia. He walked the whole 50 miles. He was worn out and hungry when he arrived. He spent his last coins on some bread. As he walked through the city, he was dirty, he had bread tucked under each arm, and his pockets were stuffed with his things. A lady spotted him and laughed. Her name was Deborah Read. Years later, Deborah became Ben's wife!

After having a chance to rest,

Ben looked for printing jobs. Samuel Keimer liked his work and hired him at his print shop. Samuel even found Ben a place to stay. The house was owned by Deborah Read's father.

> "While we may not be able to control all that happens to us, **we can control what happens inside us.**"

In 1724, just a year after arriving in colonial Philadelphia, life for Ben was finally going well. He had a roof over his head and a good job, and the people in the city liked him. Even the **governor**, Sir William Keith, got to know him and enjoyed his company. He was impressed with Ben's skill at writing and printing. He told Ben he would buy him a printing press so he could give him government work. Ben just needed to go to London to get the press and bring it back to Philadelphia.

Ben was excited to have the governor's help and to get his own press. It was a dream come true. In 1724, 18-year-old Ben set off for London very excited about his future!

## An American in London

It took Ben more than two months to sail to London. When he arrived, he found out that the governor hadn't sent money for the printing press after all! Ben had almost no money. Without the governor's loan, he could not buy the press and could not sail back home. He had to find work

right away. He found a job at a London printing house and a place to stay.

Everything Ben tried, he worked hard at. He learned as much as he could about printing and wrote his first essay. He felt proud to be in the mother country of the colonies. London was a big city with a lot to do. In the beginning of his time in London, Ben spent his money as fast as he earned it on nights out with friends. Later, he learned to save his money so he could return to Philadelphia.

### JUMP IN THE THINK TANK

Can you imagine what it would be like to go alone to a different country like Ben did? What things would be scary about it? What things would be exciting?

When he wasn't working, Ben spent time attending plays, reading, **debating** with friends, and swimming in the Thames River. One time he swam more than three miles! Twenty-year-old Ben enjoyed teaching some of his friends to swim and thought about opening his own swimming school in London. His skills

later earned him a spot in the International Swimming Hall of Fame!

Ben made many friends in London. One was a man named Thomas Denham. Thomas owned a business back in Philadelphia. He invited Ben to come back to Philadelphia and work for him at his new store. Ben missed being in America. He had been in London for a year and a half. In 1726, he boarded a ship and headed home.

**WHEN?**

| 1724 | 1726 |
|---|---|
| Ben sails to London. | Ben leaves London to go back to Philadelphia. |

# CHAPTER 4

# MAKING HIS MARK

## Master Printer

When Ben arrived back in Philadelphia, he started working for Thomas Denham right away. In 1729, he had earned enough money to finally open his own print shop! Ben's hard work was paying off. Only a year after opening, he began publishing his own newspaper. He called it *The Pennsylvania Gazette*.

Ben's newspaper was full of firsts. He created the first cartoons and maps to appear in a paper in colonial America. He also wrote jokes and stories. If there was nothing to report, he made up his own news and letters to the editor using fake names! One of his fake names was Anthony Afterwit. "Mr. Afterwit" wrote funny stories about married life.

Besides buying the print shop and starting his newspaper, Ben accomplished more as a young man. In 1730, he married Deborah Read and had two children with her—Frankie in 1732 and Sarah in 1743. Ben also had an older son whom he raised with Deborah. His name was William.

Ben and Deborah used part of their home as a shop to sell things like books, maps, coffee, paper, ink, and Josiah's soaps. One of the best-selling items was something called an almanac. Almanacs were booklets that shared weather information for the whole year, a calendar, sayings, and other helpful or fun information. In 1732, they began to sell *Poor Richard's Almanack*, and it became very popular. The author was listed as Richard Saunders, but it was written by none other than Ben Franklin himself!

| MYTH | FACT |
| --- | --- |
| Ben Franklin was always against **slavery**. | During his lifetime, Ben sometimes owned **enslaved people**. He also advertised the sale of them in his newspapers. |

Ben served his colony well, but he did not always treat all people equally. He owned **enslaved people** for many years. It wasn't until later in his life that he realized how wrong he was and became a powerful voice against **slavery.**

## Mr. Philadelphia

The people of Philadelphia liked Ben. He led a group of men called the Junto Club. They worked together to figure out ways to make their city better. As you know, Ben loved books. Back in the 1700s, books were very expensive and hard to get. Many people owned a Bible and an almanac but very few other books. Ben didn't think this was fair. He wanted everyone to have a chance to read lots of books. With the Junto Club's help, he gathered a collection of books for people to share. This collection became the country's first public library—the Library Company of Philadelphia.

Next, Ben wanted to find a way to help save citizens' homes from fires. Together with other Junto members, Ben organized the first **volunteer** fire department in 1736—the Union Fire Company.

## JUMP IN THE THINK TANK

Ben Franklin only went to school for two years. How do you think he knew how to start all of these important services and help so many people?

In the 1730s, people wrote letters to stay in touch. Ben thought communication was very important and knew he could find ways to get mail where it was going faster than the weeks and months it was taking. In 1737, Ben became Philadelphia's postmaster and improved mail delivery so it took half the amount of time.

> "When you're good to others, you're best to yourself."

Ben also wanted to make sure that kids' time in school wasn't cut short like his was. He started the Academy of Philadelphia, where boys and girls could attend school for free. It later became the University of Philadelphia. In 1751, Ben helped start the country's first hospital that treated people even if they could not pay.

By the time he was 42 years old, Ben had made enough money to sell the print shop. He wanted time to study, read, write, and think about more ways to help the people around him.

## WHEN?

**1728** Ben opens his own printing business.

**1730** Ben marries Deborah Read.

**1736** Ben starts the first volunteer fire company in America.

**1737** Ben becomes the postmaster of Philadelphia.

**1749** Ben founds the Academy of Philadelphia.

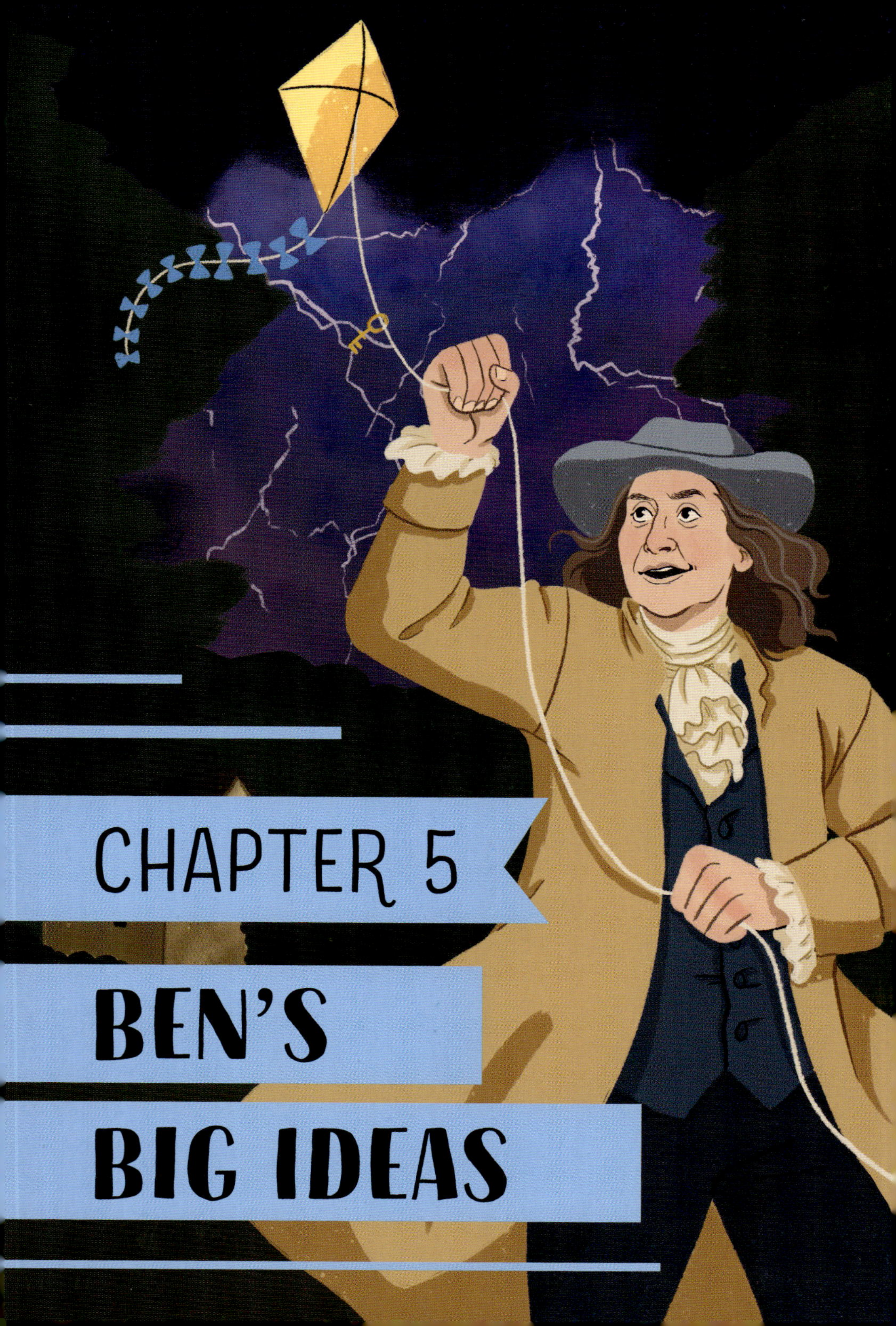

## CHAPTER 5

# BEN'S BIG IDEAS

# Ben, Scientist and Inventor

Ben's mind never rested. One of Ben's interests was science. He loved to study how things worked and invent things based on what he learned. In 1741, Ben figured out a way to heat homes better. He created a stove that used less wood than a fireplace and kept the heat inside the house. It was called the Franklin Stove.

After he **retired**, Ben took an interest in **electricity**. He thought that lightning might actually be electricity, so he tried an **experiment** with a kite during a storm. He knew lightning often struck metal, so he put a metal rod on the kite. He also tied an iron key to the string. When the kite was high in the sky, electricity from the lightning in the clouds traveled down the string to the key. When Ben put his hand too close to the key, he got a shock!

After this experiment, Ben had an idea for an invention that would keep lightning from causing house fires. He figured out that if a metal rod was put at a building's highest point, lightning would hit that instead of the roof. Ben's lightning rods saved many homes and businesses from being destroyed in fires.

## MYTH & FACT

**MYTH:** Benjamin Franklin discovered electricity.

**FACT:** Greeks noticed static electricity more than 2,000 years ago!

## Just Send Ben!

Pennsylvania, where Ben lived, was owned by and named after the British Penn family. In 1754, France and the indigenous, or native, people living in America were battling England for control of the colonies. The Penn family wanted to control Pennsylvania, but they wanted the colonists to pay for supplies and troops during the war. The colonists asked Ben to convince the British government to force the Penns to pay the money. In 1757, Ben went to England with his son William. It took Ben three years to convince the king of England to force the Penns to pay, but he finally agreed.

England won the war, but it had borrowed money from banks to pay for it. Now, England needed to pay that money back. So England made the colonies pay **taxes** on English newspapers and other paper products. It would use this tax money to pay back the money it owed.

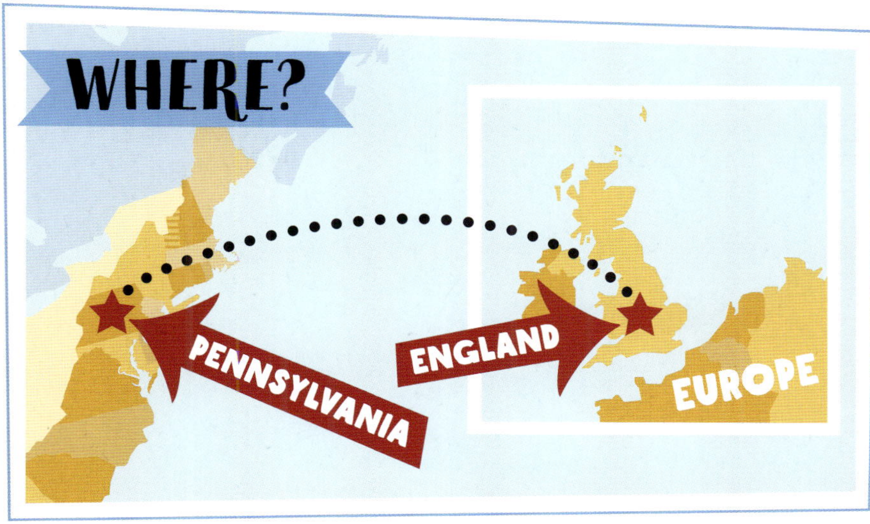


When Ben found out how upset the colonists were about this, he was in England again on another matter for his colony. Ben wrote about the unfair taxes in the English papers and talked to the English government. He got England's attention, and it stopped the tax. This success didn't last long, though. Soon, England came up with even more taxes.

In 1774, Deborah passed away unexpectedly. William blamed Ben for being gone so long. This caused bad feelings between William and Ben.

## JUMP IN THE THINK TANK

Why do you think it was necessary for Ben to travel all the way to England each time an important issue needed to be solved?

Trouble was also brewing between England and the colonists. In 1775, Ben finally headed back home, but knew he might be coming home to a war.

## WHEN?

| Ben goes to England to speak for the people of Pennsylvania. | Ben returns to Pennsylvania. | Ben goes back to England. | Ben returns to Pennsylvania. |
|---|---|---|---|
| **1757** | **1762** | **1764** | **1775** |

# CHAPTER 6

# REVOLUTION!

## Founding Father

Ben was right. By the time he arrived in Philadelphia, the **Revolutionary War** had started between England and the colonies. It was a **revolution**! Ben was only home for a few days before he was asked to speak for the state of Pennsylvania—again! This time he would stay in America and become a **delegate**—a person asked to speak for the group—to the **Continental Congress**. Every colony except Georgia sent delegates to the meeting.

The First Continental Congress met when Ben was still in England. It tried to find ways to reason with England about its unfair taxes. Once small battles in the colonies got worse and turned into war, the Second Continental Congress was formed. The delegates' job was to decide if they should make an agreement with England about taxes or if they should try to break free from England and rule themselves. Ben believed the colonies should be free of England's rule.

While Ben was trying to help the colonists unite *against* England, his son, William, sided with **loyalists**. The loyalists were united *with* England. This caused more disagreements between Ben and his son. Ben was sad that they couldn't agree. When William was eventually put in jail for his loyalty to the crown, Ben didn't help get him out.

JUMP
-IN THE-
THINK TANK

Do you think it was fair for England to make the colonists pay a tax for the things they bought from it? Why or why not?

At the Second Continental Congress, Ben and four other men—Thomas Jefferson, John Adams, Robert Livingston, and Roger Sherman—were asked to work on a Declaration of Independence. This important document explained how the colonies planned to form their own nation without England's rule. On July 4, 1776, the

delegates voted on and passed the Declaration of Independence. That date became the country's birthday. America declared that it would be an **independent nation**. They would need to fight England to make it happen.

## Ben Abroad, Again

The fight against England wouldn't be easy. America didn't have money, a strong army, or supplies. Can you guess who Congress asked for help? Ben! Its members asked him to travel to France. They wanted Ben to ask the French government to join their side in the war.

> There never was a good war or a bad peace.

The French people liked Ben. They already knew about his inventions and enjoyed his writing. Unfortunately, they didn't think the new United States was strong enough to beat the English. France decided to secretly send guns and money to the colonies because they didn't want England to know they were helping. It took years for Ben to talk the French

into signing papers to help in an **official** way. They finally signed the papers after they heard that the colonies won the Battles of Saratoga in 1777 against English troops.

France helped out in a big way with money, troops, ships, and weapons. In 1781, the large, all-powerful British army surrendered. America had won! Ben missed his family and wanted to head home, but Congress asked him to stay in France. Its members knew he would be the best person to work out a peace agreement

that England, America, and France would all be happy with. They were correct. With Ben's wisdom and talent for working with people, the **treaty** was signed in 1783. The war was finally over.

In 1785, Ben was ready to return to America. He decided to go to England first to see his son William. Ben was 79 years old. He hoped that he and William would become close again. Sadly, they could not find a way to accept each other's differences. Finally, Ben headed home to America to receive his hero's welcome.

## WHEN?

| 1776 | 1778 | 1783 | 1785 |
|---|---|---|---|
| The Declaration of Independence is signed. | Ben convinces France to help America in the war. | Ben writes a peace treaty between America and England. | Ben returns to America. |

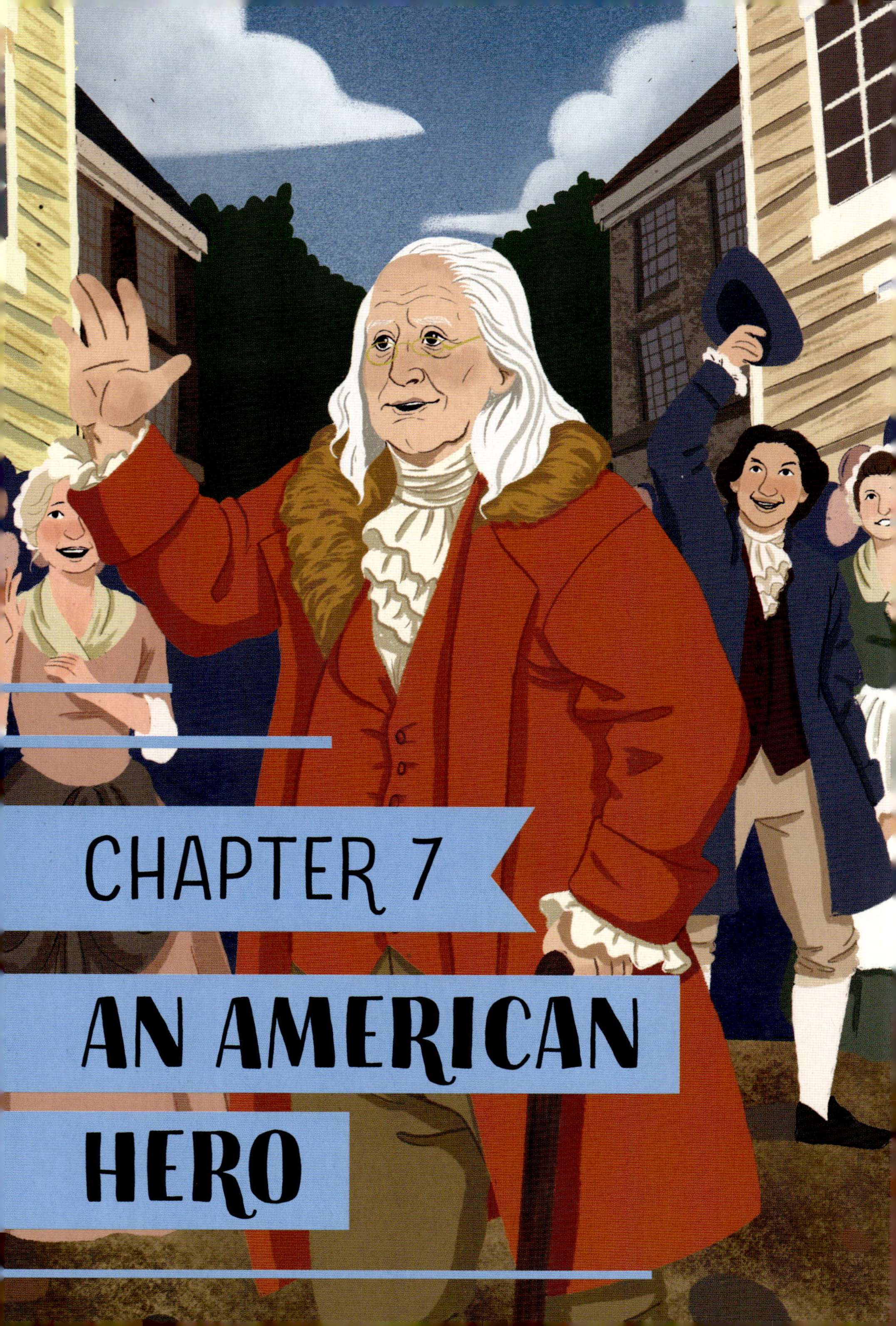

# CHAPTER 7

# AN AMERICAN HERO

## Homecoming

Ben thought he'd be coming home to a quiet retirement. When his boat docked at Market Street—where he had started off as a runaway at age 17—he got a big welcome! There were cannons firing, bells ringing, speeches, and celebrations. The people of Philadelphia were happy their hero was home.

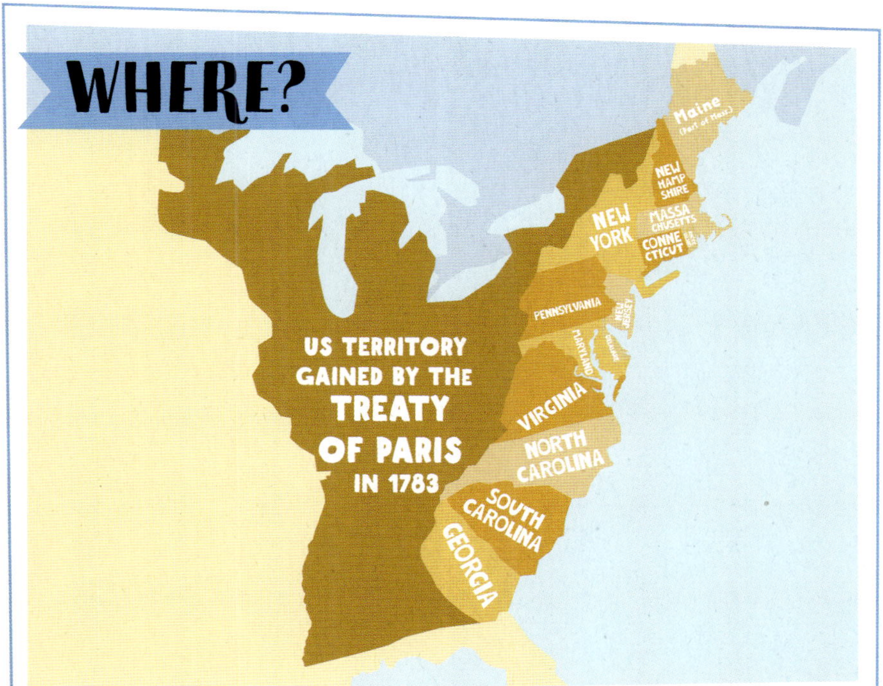

## JUMP IN THE THINK TANK

When Ben finally got back to America after being gone for 10 years, he wanted to relax. Why do you think he agreed to be the governor?

America had become its own country—the United States—with many thanks to Ben. However, there was a lot of work to do to get a government in place. The people of Pennsylvania elected Ben as their governor to lead them through this time of new beginnings.

They also asked him to be a delegate in the new government.

All of the state delegates gathered in Philadelphia to write a set of laws called the Constitution of the United States.

## MYTH & FACT

**MYTH:** Ben suggested that the turkey should be the national **symbol** on the United States' **seal**.

**FACT:** Ben actually suggested that the seal should have Moses from the Bible on it. He liked the turkey symbol, but he only shared this with his daughter in a letter.

Some states were larger than other states and wanted to have more votes. Ben came up with the idea for the government to have two parts. One part, the **House of Representatives**, would give each state a number of delegates based on how many people lived there. This let bigger states have more votes in that part of Congress. The other part, the **Senate**, would give each state the same number of delegates. After many months of meetings, the Constitution was signed in 1787.

Even though Ben was 81 years old, he still looked for ways to help others. Though Ben had once owned enslaved people, in his later years he fought against slavery. In 1787, he created and became the president of the Pennsylvania **Abolition** Society. In 1790, he asked Congress to end slavery. The Declaration of Independence states that all men are created equal. Ben wanted all enslaved people to be free and Black Americans to be treated equally. His group was the first to try to end slavery in the United States.

## The Legend Lives On

Ben kept his sense of humor throughout his life. Although he was often sick during his last few years, he enjoyed time with his grandchildren, told jokes, and had many visitors. Benjamin Franklin died on April 17, 1790, at the age of 84.

Ben's curiosity led to many inventions. He could have gotten **patents** on his inventions so other people couldn't use them for free, but Ben didn't care about being famous or having a lot of money. He cared about making life better. People trusted him because he was caring and wise. Ben could have refused to keep leaving Philadelphia and his family to help his country, but Ben felt like it was the right thing to do. Even today, he is a role model for working hard to achieve goals.

Ben was an amazing man. His talent and wisdom helped shape the country and world in so many ways. He is remembered for being a Founding Father but also for the libraries, schools, and hospitals he started and the postal and fire services he provided. There are statues of him, books and poems about him, and many places named after him.

The next time you celebrate the Fourth of July, you can remember that Ben Franklin is one of the biggest reasons Americans have an Independence Day. It's no wonder that over 20,000 people showed up to honor this great man at his funeral.

**WHEN?**

**1787** — The Constitution of the United States of America is signed.

**1790** — Ben Franklin dies on April 17 at 84 years old.

CHAPTER 8

# SO . . . WHO WAS BENJAMIN FRANKLIN?

## Challenge Accepted!

Now that you know so much about Ben's life and work, let's test your new knowledge with a little who, what, when, where, why, and how quiz. Feel free to look back in the text to find the answers if you need to, but try to remember first.

**1 When was Benjamin Franklin born?**

- A 1700
- B 1706
- C 1728
- D 1776

**2 Who was Benjamin Franklin's wife?**

- A Helen Keller
- B Eleanor Roosevelt
- C Debbie Write
- D Deborah Read

**3 What did Ben invent to help heat homes?**

- A Heating system
- B Fireplace
- C Franklin Stove
- D Franklin Furnace

## 4 Where did Ben live most of his life?

- A Philadelphia
- B Boston
- C London
- D Paris

## 5 Why did Ben run away when he was 17?

- A He wanted to travel the world.
- B His brother wasn't a kind boss.
- C He wanted to become a sailor.
- D His dad said he had to work in his candle shop.

## 6 How did Ben help America win the Revolutionary War?

- A He led the army as a general.
- B He talked France into helping with guns, supplies, and money.
- C He talked England into letting them govern themselves.
- D He had his son talk to the king of England.

## 7 What was one of Ben's inventions?

→ A The kite

→ B The refrigerator

→ C The lightning rod

→ D The printing press

## 8 What community services did Ben help create or organize?

→ A Public gardens, swimming pools, and parks

→ B Volunteer fire company, public schools, and public libraries

→ C Public streets, bridges, and highways

→ D Volunteer garbage collection, clothing charity, and a boys' outdoors club

## 9 How did Ben learn so much in his lifetime?

- A He went to school for 15 years.
- B His mom was a teacher.
- C He read a lot of books.
- D He listened to radio lessons.

## 10 Where did the states meet to write the Constitution?

- A Philadelphia
- B Boston
- C New York
- D Washington, DC

**Answers:** 1. B; 2. D; 3. C; 4. A; 5. B; 6. B; 7. C; 8. B; 9. C; 10. A

## Our World

Even though Ben was born over 300 years ago, his work changed our world today. Here are a few things we can be thankful for because of Benjamin Franklin.

- → We enjoy the freedoms we have in the United States because of the role Ben played in the Revolutionary War and the writing of the Constitution.
- → Libraries, public schools, hospitals, and post offices were all started because of Ben's ideas to improve life for people.
- → Ben's inventions and experiments with electricity led to even more discoveries in science.

# JUMP IN THE THINK TANK FOR MORE!

One of Ben's quotes was "If you would not be forgotten, as soon as you are dead and rotten, either write things worth reading, or do things worth writing." He was talking about being remembered for what you've done in your lifetime. Ben definitely won't be forgotten!

→ What do you think America would be like if people like Ben Franklin hadn't fought for independence from England?

→ Ben enjoyed writing and was good at it. What do you think would have happened if he had stayed in the printing business for his whole life?

→ What can you learn from Ben's curiosity about the world and his love for learning? What are you curious about? What would you like to learn how to do?

# Glossary

**abolition:** The ending of something, such as a law, policy, or practice

**apprentice:** Someone who works for another person to learn that person's job

**colony:** Land that is owned by a country, usually a country that is far away. People who live in a colony are **colonists**. More than one colony are **colonies**.

**Constitution of the United States:** A document written in 1787 right after the United States first became a country, which states the basic laws, instructions, and rules for how the country must be run

**Continental Congress:** A meeting of delegates from the colonies during the Revolutionary War

**debating:** Arguing about a specific topic

**Declaration of Independence:** The 1776 document announcing that the American colonies were a separate country, no longer part of England

**delegate:** Someone who represents other people at a meeting

**electricity:** A form of energy that comes from charged particles

**enslaved people:** People forced into slavery; also known as slaves

**experiment:** A procedure that scientists perform to try to make a discovery or prove a theory

**Founding Father:** A member of the group of leaders who united the 13 colonies, led them in their fight for independence from England, and helped establish a government for the new United States of America

**government:** The system of rules and people that manage a country, state, city, or local community

**governor:** Leader of a state government or colony

**House of Representatives:** A part of the United States' government that has a number of delegates based on how many people live in each state

**independent nation:** A country that is not under another country's control

**invention:** Something new that has never been made before

**legend:** Someone who is famous for something they have done

**lightning rod:** A piece of metal used on a building to direct lightning to the ground

**loyalists:** Colonists who supported the British during the Revolutionary War

**official:** When something is recognized as real and approved

**patent:** A legal document that gives someone the right to make, use, or sell an invention and prevents others from copying it

**port:** A town or city along the water where ships dock

**publish:** To make a public announcement, usually in a newspaper or other publication

**retired:** To quit working and not go back

**revolution:** To fight against the ruling government

**Revolutionary War:** A war from 1775 to 1783 that led to America's independence from England

**seal:** An official mark showing something is approved or real

**Senate:** A part of the United States' government that has two delegates for each state

**slavery:** A system in which people are treated like property and forced to work against their will for no pay

**symbol:** An object taking the place of an idea of another object. Symbols usually stand for or mean something.

**tax:** Money the government collects in addition to what something costs

**treaty:** An agreement between countries

**volunteer:** A person who participates in something without being paid

# Bibliography


Davidson, Margaret. *The Story of Benjamin Franklin: Amazing American.* Milwaukee: Gareth Stevens Publishing, 1988.

Fish, Bruce, and Becky Durost Fish. *Benjamin Franklin: American Statesman, Scientist, and Writer.* Philadelphia: Chelsea House Publishers, 1999.

Fradin, Dennis Brindell. *Who Was Ben Franklin?* New York: Grosset & Dunlap, 2002.

Giblin, James Cross. *The Amazing Life of Benjamin Franklin.* New York: Scholastic, 2006.

Roop, Peter, and Connie Roop. *In Their Own Words: Benjamin Franklin.* New York: Scholastic, 2001.

Uglow, Loyd. *Benjamin Franklin: You Know What to Say.* Houston: Advance Publishing, 2001.

# About the Author

**SHANNON ANDERSON** has taught for 25 years, from first grade all the way up through the college level. She also loves writing books for kids and teachers. Shannon received her bachelor's degree at none other than Franklin College, named after Ben himself! She has served as the regional advisor for the Society of Children's Book Writers and Illustrators, and was named one of the Top 10 Teachers by the *Today Show* in 2019. To find out more about Shannon or her books, you can visit her website at **ShannonIsTeaching.com**.

# About the Illustrator

**STEFFI WALTHALL** is an illustrator and character designer who has always been inspired by strong, fearless women, whether in history or in fiction. Steffi loves human-centric stories and creating images that celebrate and embrace diversity (and usually include a lady with a sword). When not working on a project, she can be found searching for inspiration in a book or out in nature with her Polaroid camera looking for another story to begin.